CHRONICLES OF

BLACK SELF-HATRED

By Asafo Chuma Asafo

PRINTED AND PUBLISHED BY:

LEGATEE INK PUBLISHING

1623 Dalton Street #14939

Cincinnati, Ohio 45250

Layout & Illustrations Queen Tahiyrah

© LEGATEE INK PUBLISHING 2018

*** INTRODUCTION ***

As a TRIED & TRUE (preemptive) maneuver, whenever and wherever whites have moved to colonize/enslave and or otherwise subdue non-white peoples (for protracted exploitation), They would first, through their literature, media, social-science, religious interpretations, etc., demonize and degrade those peoples, to make any aggressions against them seem "justifiable" even "necessary".

In Vietnam, for Instance, the Vietcong resistance fighters were called "gooks "; "slant-eyed vermin", etc.; a dehumanizing set of epithets honed & refined in the U.S.'s prior (Imperial) aggressions against the Korean peoples and the partitioning of their country to isolate the (non-cooperative) North from the (cooperative) South.

In Mogadishu, Somalia - the Afrikan natives were called "skinnies" by the white-led U.S. military invaders - with the first four letters in the name, referencing their color, a hue already presented to the world as less than the other extreme of the (racial) color' spectrum. (See the film "Blackhawk Down").

"Towel-heads" for Middle-Eastern peoples, whose overall identity, by the way, has now become one with "terrorism". And "wet-backs" and other denigrating cognomens for Spanish speaking peoples.

As for Blacks: "niggers, "coons", "monkeys" and whatever else whites decided to call Blacks, including "boy" (for Black Men). Far beyond mere name-calling, however, is the institutionalizing of racial hatred & discrimination through policies & laws, i.e., Black-Code laws and Jim Crowism (both old & new) which created the status quo of white superiority/Black inferiority. And this status quo has been morphed into the very fabric of Amerikkkan society.

Interestingly though, is its ability to conceal itself behind the veils of nuance & subtleties, to evade definitive detection while maintaining its evil effect no less. In this way, the racist power holders are able to monopolize not only the language (including the clever code words) embedded in discriminatory practices, but the actual framework or context in which it Is even to be mentioned (or not).

For example, when the white police apparatus shoots an unarmed Black kid in Ferguson, Missouri, or strangle a Black man, to death for selling loose cigarettes on a New York street, or brutally pummel a middle-aged defenseless Black woman on a California highway, for merely walking in traffic, whites immediately retreat behind the facade of "Colorblindness" while at the same time "criminalizing" the victims of this police terror; as a tacit way of implying that they "Got What They Deserved". But the reality is, Black life has no value in white Amerikkka!

Tragically, Blacks seem to share this sentiment, as displayed in the virtual normalization of Black-on-Black violence and the fluent use of the word "NIGGER/ 'NIGGA" when referring to one another, as "bitch" (when referring to Black women), indicating the internalization of their own oppression.

That whites have positioned themselves as the most beautiful and most intelligent people in the world, thus the (supreme) authority on everything of social/human consequence, isn't the problem. the problem is that Black people believe it! So, this small book comes to the hood to expose and debunk these fallacies, as they have taken up residency in the minds of Blacks; not to convince whites of who they are and how they should recognize their wrongs. They already recognize them; and they will never change their ways, only reinvent them to maintain their rulership over everyone else. So, this discussion is for Blacks only.

We will leave the 'politically correct', half-hearted, apologetic' mumbo-jumbo to the "negro" politicians, as their wishful thinking for "Racial Equality" gets a joy ride on the rollercoaster of (conditional) "acceptance" by whites. This book is for the Blacks who are sick & tired of tip-toeing through the minefield of deceptive rhetoric, laid down by whites, and living in the shadow of perpetual suspicion and condemnation.

Moreover, our aim is to cut through the static of who Blacks have been led to believe they are, by whites; and the lowly position Blacks have been stuck in for centuries, and to return to the source of our true selves. We are not "Niggers/Niggas", "Bitches" or any other pejorative adjectives ascribed to us by whites.

WE ARE AFRIKAN!

~IRON EYE~

***THE NIGGER FACTOR ***

"The most potent weapon in the hands of the oppressor is the mind of the oppressed."

-WARRIOR-ANCESTOR STEVE BIKO-

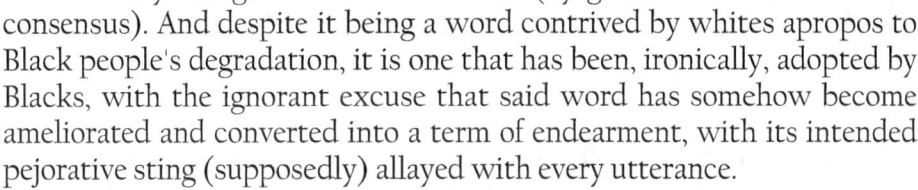

WITHOUT QUESTION, the word NIGGER is the most racially charged word in existence (by global consensus). And despite it being a word contrived by whites apropos to Black people's degradation, it is one that has been, ironically, adopted by Blacks, with the ignorant excuse that said word has somehow become ameliorated and converted into a term of endearment, with its intended pejorative sting (supposedly) allayed with every utterance.

The excuses for failing to extirpate this word (by Blacks) are as lame as those used by many blacks to shirk their inherent duty to confront the purveyors of the word; not only for the rhetorical venom contained in its definition, but primarily for its institutional and sociological ramifications.

While it is true that there's power in words, it is the power of those who control the very fate of Black people that Blacks should concern themselves with. However, there's a major glitch in the thought process of Blacks, which precludes them from confronting their true enemy; and that is, they have been programmed (by their enemy) to hate themselves!!

To see a whole entire race of people completely removed from their culture, and deeply submerged in a psychological vat of self-hatred, must be the most profound phenomenon of the 21st century (or any other century). This colossal tragedy is doubly compounded by the fact that not only are they in denial of their (mental) condition of self-hatred, but they have even been programmed to LOVE those who made them this way.

This is actually the bane of Black peoples' dilemma. After being stolen from their original homeland (Afrika), having their self-image, languages, cultural customs, etc. ripped from them, and sub-assimilated (by osmosis) into a foreign (European) culture, the result is the birth of the NIGGER.

The NIGGER is the manufactured product of white supremacy and white domination, to serve their intents & purposes. The NIGGER was created for the specific and expressed purpose of negating any forward progress of Blacks, toward any modicum of self-worth, self-determination, etc. The NIGGER is, in summation, wired to self-destruct.

The fluent use of the word NIGGER and other related derogatory terms, by Blacks are mere (verbal) indices of their overall mental death. Still, to focus on the use of the word NIGGER = NIGGA (no matter the variation), without equally addressing every form of, what **Brother Akil** aptly termed "Niggativity", then the entire approach is inane - as Black self-detestation is manifested in many other ways besides its verbal iterations.

For instance, recently while watching a program promoting "Racial Harmony" in Amerikkka, I witnessed a Black woman passionately decry the use of the word "NIGGER" while at the same time openly praising the benevolence of the European creed (as it relates to Blacks & other non-Whites) - all the while donning a blonde wig and blue contact lenses. Point being, this ostensible contradiction among others, is pervasive.

Black people must come to the full realization that they cannot effectively contend with, and simultaneously worship & emulate, their enemy, the very source of their (mental) condition of self-hatred. There are no gray areas in war; especially one waged on the psycho-cultural frontier. Either youlre a friend or foe.

And Black people cannot afford to move tepidly when it comes to this level of contention. For the fate of a people is at stake. After all, the oppressor didn't half-step when he implemented the (mental) weapon of self-hatred, which was artificially inseminated into the minds of Black people (as a whole). One must admit that it is an ingenious, albeit evil & clever, tactic (in the context of mental war) to cause a people to hate themselves and love their enemy.

It gives full meaning to the axiom: "He who controls your thinking ultimately controls your actions." The gross fratricidal behavior and the widespread emulation of whites and their overall culture is directly and inextricably connected to this vanquished mind state. And though many Blacks openly acknowledge that Blacks are in a state of mental torpor, they tend to stop short of contributing the creation of said mind state to the white oppressor; for it draws the line in the sand of us against them.

Ironically, whites are already functioning in this mode (always have been); although concealed behind a smile and an unequivocal denial. There are even some Blacks who use their (individual) "Friendships" and other quasi relationships with whites to try to explain away the hegemonic nature of their overall culture (as it ill-affects Blacks and other non-whites, globally). These are those Blacks who are most susceptible to, what our Warrior-Scholar Wade Nobles calls: "Conceptual Incarceration", whereby their concept of reality is confined to the self-serving, European version of reality.

Wade Nobles

Imprisoned within this framework, they speak and function within a sanitized "politically correct" context when attempting to address the age-old "race problem", which automatically forbids them from placing the blame where it rightfully belongs.

In fact, it is this class of confused "negroes" who are fond of uttering: "We can't keep blaming the white man for our problems", as if our Maafa (the on-going destruction of Afrikan peoples) has ended and the (blame game) has simply reached ad nauseam (as far as they're concerned); or, maybe it is a constant reminder of their own betrayal. Whatever the case, it only serves the continuity of white domination.

THE BLACK MERITOCRACY CLASS

"No amount of Individual achievement or the gaining of personal acceptance by whites on the part of Black Individuals, will remove from them the stigma of their membership in a powerless race."

- WARRIOR-SCHOLAR-ANCESTOR DR. AMOS N. WILSON-

IN a capitalist-imperialist society· like Amerikkka, money, material possessions, "prestige" and ultimately the acceptance and approval of the modern white slave master trumps real, authentic race loyalty. And this fact is on full display with Black public figures (especially politicians) sports figures, entertainers and the like. These (among others) represent the MERITOCRACY CLASS. For these are the "negroes" that are so blinded by their sub-integrationist, individualistic ambitions and aspirations within the matrix that they have become the modern helots of the white creators & controllers of the matrix.

And they hold an odious contempt for those (other Blacks) who are not in compliance with the "system". They sincerely, although ignorantly, believe that they have "arrived" or "made it". They are, in effect, walking corpses, completely bereft of their Afrikan (cultural) life, and are therefore animated by Eurocentric views & precepts, thereby precluded from the ability to even think a thought outside of the white oppressor's conceptual restraints.

Colin Powell, Armstrong Williams, Clarence Thomas, Condoleezza Rice, et al. are just a few of the most visible examples of this class of treasonous "negroes". They couldn't speak a word in favor of their own people in public, even if they wanted to, from fear of being summarily disposed of by their modern white masters. They represent the illusion that race doesn't matter (in racist Amerikkka): that this is the "melting pot" where all cultures are "equally" meshed into one. Yet their very rhetoric (and actions) with regards to peoples and cultures other than Europeans' are invariably subject to gross prevarications, and ultimately sub-assimilation (under the boot of white rule).

In reality, for any Black or non-white person or group to excel (unopposed) in this white dominated society, they have to be a loyal proponent of the cultural creed of white supremacy. The very behavior of (mentally) enslaved "negroes" is a conspicuous spectacle of affectation, a modern tap-dance (to shamelessly please & appease white folks). In fact, white folks wouldn't have it any other way. They fear REAL Black men & women.

And the only REAL Black men & women in this wasteland are those who stand on their own cultural) two feet regardless of the opposition. Our warrior-scholar Walter Rodney once quipped: "The only great men (and women) among a poor and oppressed people are those who fight to destroy their oppressor." Moreover, the only Black men & women QUALIFIED to destroy their oppressor (and his NIGGER FACTOR) in both word and in (dirty) deed, are those whose (Black) souls are unsold to the white oppressor.

This is one of the reasons why the white oppressor has a fetish for docile, non-threatening, obsequious "negroes ". And said "negroes" are granted access to flourish within the parameters of "Pop Culture" i.e., Television, Music, Media, Politics and such. And since the oppressor ultimately controls these mediums (thus the perceptions of those influenced by them), he sees to it that the only images of Blacks portrayed to the public at large are those of homosexuals, servants/slaves, pimps & hoes, (Amerikkkan) gangsters, comedians, drug dealers, buffoons, informants, political conformists and the like.

The white oppressor especially gets a kick out of Black men being portrayed as women. In fact, one of the main reasons why Dave Chapelle was demonized and ostracized by his white bosses is because he left his popular show, opting out of a lucrative contract renewal, at the apex of the show's popularity & profitability, in protest of being pressured by the Comedy Central network brass to portray a woman in at least one of his skits. And understanding the politics of imagery, especially as it pertains to Blacks and other nonwhites, Chapelle voiced his disdain. In response, the white bosses began to spread rumors that Dave Chapelle had gone insane, was addicted to crack, and a host of other slanderous aspersions - simply because he had the will & dignity to walk away from a multi-million-dollar contract.

Ironically, his white bosses went so far as to name the so-called "great" comedians who had done it, e.g., Flip Wilson (Geraldine); Martin Lawrence (Sha nay-nay, Big Momma's House); Eddie Murphy (Nutty Professor) Jamie Foxx (In Living Color's Wanda), et al. which prompted Dave Chapelle to retort: "My point, exactly."

Even those blacks who claim a sense of cultural con-sciousness come with a disclaimer, to remain in the good graces of the modern slave master; this especially applies to those in the entertainment business. Take for instance, the popular rapper Nas' music video for the song "I know I can (Be what I wanna be) wherein, after eloquently and very poetically delineating the greatness of Afrikans (in antiquity), replete with a compelling vis-ual limn of the pyramids and other ancient and tradition-

Dave Chapelle

al artifacts & imagery, in an effort to connect todayls Black youth to their cultural core, he antithetically displays the words on a shirt hels wearing, at the end of the video that reads: "I AM THE AMERICAN DREAM", which in effect cancelled out the original message.

It is this kind of ambiguity and half-heartedness that suspends any forward movement, because it says on the one hand, that, you should know your (Afrikan) history & culture, hence your Afrikan self; but at the same time strive for the Amerikkkan dream, which treasonously ignores the fact that Amerikkka is the prime culprit in not only killing the dreams & aspira-tions of Afrikans, but murdering Afrikans themselves.

Flip Wilson as
Geraldine

History has shown that those who speak outside of the oppressor's conceptual (cultural) credo (without a dis-claimer) are penalized. Case in point: When former basketball star Tim Hardaway was asked the question - considering a (lesser known) basketball player's an-nouncement that he was gay - how did he feel about gays in the sport of basketball, Hardaway openly de-clared that he didnlt approve of it, and that he prefers not to be around them. Tim made the mistake of think-

Nas

ing that they wanted his honest answer. Well, he soon discovered other-wise. The white owned & operated media, at the behest of the GAY & LESBIAN ALLIANCE (The Homosexual Mafia) and ilk, jumped all over him; and even pressured the Miami Heat power holders to relieve him of his front office job. And of course, white folks (and their colorful clones), via their far-reaching media apparatus, painted him to be the pariah. Needless to say, under such pressure, Hardaway immediately apologized and quickly back-pedaled from his original position.

Europeans and Afrikans operate from two different ethos patterns. Homosexuality is endemic to European culture not Afrikan culture. Undoubtedly, Hardaway was speaking (perhaps unconsciously) from his (Afrikan) ethos when he spoke his mind. The problem with a lot of Blacks is that they (erroneously) think that all peoples (Black, white & otherwise) are all just parts of the same hue-man family, thus sharing the same cultural ethos; when in reality, nothing could be more farther from the truth.

Hardaway

The Black actor Isaiah Washington, formerly of the hit TV drama (GREY' S ANATOMY) is another casualty of the European-headed homosexual mafia. One day while on the set of the show he purportedly got into a confrontation with one of his (gay) white cast mates whom he reportedly called a "faggot". Needless to say, the entire white cast (and the few other "negroes 11) turned against him. And he was summarily terminated. But not before he was painted as "The Problem".

Isaiah Washington

The sad part was when they convinced the poor brother that he was WRONG. Even compelled him to make a Public Service Announcement (PSA) denouncing "gay bashing", And still that wasn't enough. They sent him to get "psychological treatment II, to exorcise him of his "hate' (if he expected to ever work in tinsel-town again).

Clearly, if members of the Black meritocracy class wish to maintain their vaunted status and achievements they can NEVER go against white folks or their cultural imperatives (even though Europeans routinely disregard and disrespect the cultural imperatives of Afrikans, daily). Late night talk show host, Arsenio Hall. learned this lesson early on, when the homosexual mafia and the Zionist oppressors forced the cancellation of his popular show, for inviting "controversial" Black Muslim

Arsenio Hall

Leader Minister Louis Farrakhan on to galvanize support for the then up -coming Million Man March.

The white oppressor doesn't tolerate any strong Black images being portrayed to the world; at least not minus an equally strong disclaimer, to diminish its validity. The oppressor figures that white power & Black power cannot occupy the same space at the same time (at least not within the context of European culture). 50 vanquished Blacks are the only Blacks white folks "like".

They readily provide a forum for said vanquished Blacks to display their (introjected) self-hatred and (acquired) ignorance, on shows like Maury Povich, Jerry Springer, et al. while at the same time bolstering the oppressor's claims of "superiority". So, it is obvious that the solutions to the problems plaguing Blacks (collectively) cannot be expected to come from the Black meritocracy class sector. For they are disqualified, by their vanquished mind state and their sub-integration into the capitalist imperial system, to help their own people.

Oprah Winfrey epitomizes this meritocratic designation. She embodies the proverbial axiom: 'What does it profit a man (or woman) who gains the whole world (acceptance by Europeans), but loses his/her own (cultural) soul?' She apparently thinks that her financial stature (within the capitalist construct) compensates for her cultural ineptitude. Therefore, she openly advocates euro-centric ideals.

This is best displayed on her popular daytime talk show, where nothing of real, tangible substance (as far as Blacks are concerned) is ever discussed. Sure, if a topic (of significance) is prevalent in the public domain she'll cover it; but only after it is thoroughly filtered through a euro-centric sieve. In the wake of the Don Imus,

Michael Richards (of Seinfeld fame) and Dog (The Bounty Hunter's) racist tirades, respectively, she chose to attack Hip-Hop as a way of skirting the real issue. But this isn't new. Back in '92, in the wake of the LA rebellion, resulting from the Rodney King verdict, she eventually covered the story; But she labeled the segment "Black Rage" and mainly centered on the so-called "looting" & "rioting".

The fact that a klan of evil white racist police officers had gotten off after beating an unarmed Black man nearly to death (before the entire world)

was treated as a mere incidental. The 'White Rage' that precipitated the entire ordeal was conveniently overlooked.

Incidentally, this was around the time when she was starving herself to fit into the physical paragon of white imagery. The fat Black girl was (and still is) unacceptable within the self-serving quintessence of the prevailing Eurocentric definition of beauty. However, when she couldn't meet the weight criteria she finally settled on having her (Afrikan) nose shaved down a bit. And she generally promotes the ruling European agenda.

She endorses white folks' books, movies, fashion and every other aspect of Europeans' life styles, including their decadent proclivities. She once even stated that the smartest man she knows is John Travolta (a white man). She deliberately distances herself from authentic Afrikan-centered scholars (because white don't approve), while she, conversely, endorses Dr. Phil (a white man).

John Travolta &

Oprah Winfrey

Yet she (arrogantly) assumes the authority to speak on the language in Hip-Hop, violence in the Black colony, the use of the word NIGGER (by Blacks), etc. And even then, her primary aim is to appease her white audience, white sponsors and white "friends". She is, in reality, not qualified to speak on anything concerning the black colony, for the simple fact that she is strictly verboten, by her own fear, ignorance and ostensible self-hatred, to point out the (euro-centric) pathogen that causes it all, to begin with.

Dr. Phil &

Oprah Winfrey

Moreover, she apparently believes that her (individual) riches and "prestige' (in the matrix) has elevated her above and beyond her inherent obligation to the collective struggle of Blacks here in the hells of Amerikkka and in the Diaspora. Sure, she may be able to purchase a whole host of "friends" and other (diversionary) trinkets, but no amount of money can buy her self-love!

Harvey Weinstein

& Oprah Winfrey

And the All-Girls academy she erected in Azania (so-called South Africa), though believed to be a sincere gesture on her part, is suspect nonetheless. For to offer Afrikans any kind of "education" divorced from an authentic Afrika centered curriculum, is merely a grand exercise in self-defeat. After all, what good does it serve an Afrikan to be taught an "education" that is primarily geared toward the ultimate service to, and the maintenance of, the apparatus of white domination? This is - in summation - the etiology of the disease of self-hatred which marks the overall powerlessness of Afrikans the world over.

In this vein, **Warrior-Ancestor-Scholar John Henrik Clarke** cogently points out: *"We have to realize that education has but one honorable purpose -one alone - everything else is a waste of time: that is to train the student to be a proper handler of power. Being Black and being Beautiful means nothing until ultimately, you're Black and powerful. The world is ruled by power, not Blackness and not Beautyalone)."*

Running completely counter to the above stated dictum, Blacks are, uniformly, urged by the (white) rulers of this society along with the treasonous Black meritocracy class - who have a stake in said society to support white domination (although cloaked in euphemistic terminology and proxy participation). Blacks in this white dominated society are perpetually compelled to "speak properly", "conduct themselves properly", to get a "proper education", to "obey the proper authorities" and to pretty much conform to the overall etiquette of European standards. And since "proper" is a code word for WHITE, this means that Blacks have to negate their own cultural mores; for, by their natural contrast to those of their occidental counterpart, they must be "wrong" or "improper".

And contrary to popular deception, Blacks cannot ascertain real power without first standing on their cultural foundation. The essence of one's culture naturally empowers them. It is also important to be clear that having (individual) riches doesn't constitute being powerful. There are scores of Blacks who consider themselves rich. But, how many have power? We're not speaking of the make-believe power "negroes" seem to revel in.   We mean **REAL** power!

And make no mistakes, Blacks are yearning for power; the power to rule over their own existence. And its delayed acquisition has a direct connection to why the ubiquitous "Stay in School" slogans has consistently fallen on deaf ears (in the hood), and why the school dropout rate has skyrocketed. The Black youth have come to realize that the "education" they're given (by their oppressor) is inferior and disconnected from real, tangible power. Sure, one can "learn" how to accumulate money (within the parameters of capitalism) in this society, but power seems to still be in the hands of whites.

Whenever an authentic Afrikan-centered social agenda, for the (collective) empowerment of Blacks, is formally introduced to the black colony we will see the natural genius of Blacks rise to the occasion. But until such time, we'll just continue to witness Blacks being turned in circles within the circumference of servitude and powerlessness.

And contrary to the euro-centric directed innuendo & propaganda, Black self-hatred isn't the result of some parthenogenetic apparition, where such an abnegating notion was (immaculately) conceived in the minds (or culture) of Black people (to their own detriment). Nor is it an auto-didactical manifestation where Blacks have created a doctrine of self-deprecation to facilitate their own (collective) demise.

In fact, the very (tacit) and ostensible implications of such absurdity are in line with white Amerikkka's ongoing pathology of "Blaming the Victim". And the fact that a lot of so-called "prominent" blacks acquiesce to such spurious lines of reasoning lends credence to it, which in turn disqualifies them from both (definitively) identifying, and, (decisively) contending with its euro-centric source.

Ironically, this meritocratic class of treasonous blacks, i.e., Stanley Crouch, Juan Williams, Larry Elders and a host of other white approved "neqroes " seems to be the only ones forever called in front of the oppressor's national cameras to offer their myopic, 'politically correct' views & analyses on the putrid condition of the Black colony.

Undoubtedly, the Black-on-Black violence that has become a virtual routine occurrence in the hood is the most obvious manifestation of Black self-hatred. However, the NIGGER FACTOR, as it relates to the overall disease of Black self-detestation, isn't confined to its (overt) violent manifestations alone. For it is certainly present, albeit a bit more nuanced, and in some cases, streamlined, within the entire gamut of Blacks' (influenced) behavior - which, when comprehended in the broader scope, offers a more panoramic view of the full magnitude of

Black self-hatred - in terms of its many constituent elements being equally detrimental to the overall wellbeing, resurrection and liberation of Black people.

Therefore, it isn't enough to shine a spotlight on those who act out their self-hatred in spates of fratricidal violence but neglect to give equal attention to every other aspect of it and its root causes. For it is the height of hypocrisy to see blacks, who have sold their souls to the oppressor, or who otherwise promote euro-centric ideals (in general), claim they're our leaders.

The reality is, it will take culturally conscious and committed Blacks from among the warrior class, to bring forth a new reality for our people. Afrikan-centered imperatives is the only remedy for the (mental) sickness Blacks suffer from. To continue to call upon vanquished "negroes", who function from a more refined extreme of the same strain of Black self -hatred, and who have an (illusory) stake in the capitalist matrix, further exacerbates, confounds and trivializes things, especially to the Black youth who, despite being buried in a graveyard of cultural death, can still discern hypocrisy.

The Black colony is in need of clear-cut & decisive warriors who will speak the truth, and, more importantly, practice what they preach, regardless of the circumstances or opposition. Those who will, as our warrior-scholar Dr. Amos N. Wilson once put it:

> "Knock the chip from the (oppressive) bully's shoulder .... Throw down the gauntlet
> Draw the line in the sand."

In fact, in a recent address to the Black youth, regarding the ineptitude and cowardice leadership among the (bought & paid-for) meritocracy class of Amerikkkan "negroes", Minister Louis Farrakhan boldly pointed out:

> "These weak -kneed leaders are not your defenders. If they are too weak to point out
> your enemies, they can never be your defenders."

*** THE TRAGIC MULATTO ***

"It appears that on the American social hierarchy, privilege and acceptance into the fold of the white power holders is meted out according to color gradation, with the mulatto receiving preferential favor prorata to their physical (and mental) resemblance to the white oppressor, in contrast to those with undeniably pure Afrikan blood (and cultural consciousness)."

- MCHUMA JICHO, NBLA-

FROM THE VERY inception of slavery here in North Amerikkka and throughout the Caribbean and the West Indies, there has been the so-called mulatto factor, which has been a gift and a curse. That is to say they have been used both in favor of and against the struggle of Blacks here in the western hemisphere; as well as the fact that some had effectively used it interchangeably, to gain access to the best of both worlds (so to speak). Many have, however, outright betrayed their inherent Afrikan allegiance (and identity) thus the struggle.

It is common knowledge that being Black in any society ruled & dominated by whites (and their ideals), and an overall atmosphere of contempt and hostility towards Blacks, is a daunting task by any measure. So as an escape from the rigors or dangers of merely possessing Black skin is such a society, those who could pass for white did so (and still do). Some even oscillated from one extreme to the other, to satisfy their (personal) whims. These types are described by warrior-ancestor John Henrik Clarke, as, "A drop of ink in a glass of water" where the water becomes both unsuitable for drinking, as well as unsuitable for writing, thus useless!

There was a relatively large mulatto movement in the Caribbean, in the second half of the 19th century; especially in Jamaica, where they wanted their mulatto status "legally" recognized. They (in most cases) could not be outright classified as white. But they, under no circumstances, wanted to be classified as Black. A great portion of them remained among Blacks as spies; some as revolutionaries. This color stratification made its way to the states. In Louisiana (in particular) there arose sizeable mulatto or "Creole" societies which, to this very day, are thoroughly matriculated into the ruling white social (class) structure - and would go to their graves denying their own Blackness.

Nowadays, the mulatto is more streamlined in society, but still fall under the: "If you're Black stay back; If you're Brown stick around; If you're Yellow you're mellow; If you're White you're alright I! social/racial maxim, perpetuated by the white power holders. Even the "good hair/bad-hair" myth still persists (with Blacks portrayed in the negative of course) which, in actuality- is a reversal of the psychological framework of the races. Because in reality Blacks veritably have the "good" or best hair; not as a vaunted rhetorical assertion, but as an acknowledgment of universal truth. Black people's hair is consistent with life. This is best illustrated by the fact that when Black people's hair grow it grows upward, toward the sky, displaying its strength & vitality. It is literally a living manifestation of its melanated power; in stark contrast to that of its European counterparts'. When white folks' hair grows it falls down (over their shoulders) toward the ground.

Its recessive texture, marked by a gross absence of Melanin precludes it from standing (on its own). This means that it is lifeless. This goes for their recessive (weak) eye colors as well. This helps to understand their undying commitment to the slander and overall demonization of all images (other than European), and their inherent need to superimpose their (white) images as superior to all others - over the world.

And the vanquished Blacks who have fallen for this lame trick are in perpetual retreat from their own Blackness and into the open arms of white imagery, white approval, white culture. And since European images along with their definition of beauty is the prevailing aesthetic, the mulatto, for the most part, measures their beauty (phenotypically) from the European paradigm, as opposed to their Afrikan "side". In fact, this is characteristic of our more popular mulattos, i.e., Mariah Carey, Tiger Woods, Halle Berry, et al. It is no secret that Mariah Carey carries herself like a white woman. She has openly dated white men; was even married to one (purportedly to further her singing career). And when that "arrangement' waned she switched back to Black (Nick Canon); purportedly to maintain a relevance in the music industry, in terms of pushing Black music.

Tiger Woods has publicly denounced being a Black man (even in the face of his Black father). He only dates white women (was even married to one). And he openly speaks of Black people, to his white "friends' as "Those People'

Halle Berry, in an interesting way, represents the paragon of the I tragic Mulatto'. We deduce this, based in large part, on the general responses of most men (Black & White) who almost unanimously mention her as the quintessence of "beauty" when asked to describe the ideal woman (within the context of "popular culture"). No doubt, white men are inclined to her European like features, mixed with their latent fantasies of being with a Black woman.

Mariah Carey

But this is, strangely enough, the case with a lot of Black men, as well. She certainly represents white ideals, which is reinforced by the fact that in virtually every one of her movies she's paired with a white man. And the few where she's paired with a Black man it is invariably in a negative light. She epitomizes the 'Imitation of Life' style mulatto, where her racial confusion is evinced in her "real-life' behavior. She married and quickly divorced two Black men: David Justice (of Atlanta Braves fame) and soul singer Eric Benet, respectively; And has, not surprisingly, finally moved on to white men (exclusively). she revels in the fact that she was awarded a "prestigious" Oscar for portraying what amounted to be the white man's play thing, in the film MONSTER'S BALL - where she (explicitly) allows a white man to have his way with her sexually; who happens to be the racist white prison guard who is, incidentally, the keeper of the father of her son (played by P. Diddy) who is on the prison's death row.

Tiger Woods

Halle Berry

And although it is "Just A Movie" we know that (in this world) the perception of reality is like reality itself. Halle Berry openly bases her worth and self-esteem on white approval and acceptance; for white folks' approval means more to her than that of Blacks.

Tragically, this very vanquished mind state is pervasive among all shades of Black women in the Amerikkkan society (and beyond), as it has become common to see our beautiful Black sisters forsake their natural looks in favor of the European aesthetic. It is no empty coincidence that sisters (in the public eye), i.e.., Mary J. Blige, Keyshia Cole, Eve, Beyoncé, Nicki Minaj and a host of other talented sisters find the need to wear blonde locks and such, in an industry that promotes the European image above all else; And marginalize sisters like Lauryn Hill, Angie Stone, Jill Scott, India Arie, Erykah Badu, et al.

Erykah Badu

There are no Black people in the entire universe (outside of rare cases of albinism) being born with the weak or recessive blonde hair. Blonde hair is a white thing. So, to see Blacks paying homage by emulating their historical and modern enslavers is nothing short of blasphemy, and ultimately denotes a hatred for their natural Black selves.

Angie Stone

The mulatto is subtly promoted as the solution to the "race problem", in terms of being acknowledged as "Really" Black (in an ignored reality), but representative of eurocentric thought, behavior and allegiance in the matrix of white supremacy. And since a lot of Blacks are still under the

Nicki Minaj

(psychological) spell of the European-structured thought paradigm, they are unable to discern the tricknology of the mulatto being pitched as the perfect "buffer" or "gray" representative of the two races.

This is the underlying factor in the ascension of Barack H. Obama to the U.S. presidency. On the one hand people are led to feel like they've finally gotten a "Black" president (for the "historical" novelty of it all), while the white oppressor continues the real, tangible business of white domination. Sure, they appease their "negro" constituents and the un-

Barack H. Obama

witting masses with their public farce of "racial progress" so that everyone (seemingly) gets what they want.

Beyoncé

This is one of the main hindrances to Blacks especially here in Amerikkka from establishing their own sovereign territory, wherein they can set up their own Afrikan-centered social system. Instead, they've become content with their sub-integrationist existence within the matrix of white supremacy. Some even foolishly think that they can, over time, change the hegemonic nature of whites; even though history consistently illustrates that no other non-European people have ever been "equally" integrated into any European-dominated society.

You are required to check your respective culture at the door before being admitted entry into the European matrix, which means self-negation is a prerequisite. This goes for the mulatto, too. It is important to point out that this study in the tragedy of the mulatto, as it relates to the overall discussion on self-hatred, doesn't necessarily encompass every so-called biracial person, as some of the most astute Afrikan-centered warriors are the (biological) offspring of Black & white parents, but are indubitably Afrikan!

"Integration and Amalgamation of the races are in fact exercises in fatalism and wishful thinking. Why? Because there was never a time in the history of man where slave masters of one group ever voluntarily let the other group become its equal under the same government while the slave master remained in control.

- WARRIOR ANCESTOR-SCHOLAR YOSEF BEN-JOCHANNAN-

"You are not American citizens or members of the white man's world. The only American citizens are white people who are originally from Europe. So why fight a losing battle of trying to be recognized as something you are not and never will be. I am not trying to disillusion you but merely telling you the truth."

-WARRIOR MESSENGER ELIJAH UHAMMAD -

*** MENTACIDE = FRATRICIDE ***

As STATED EARLIER, the Black-on-Black violence that has become a regular occurrence in the Black colony is the most telling manifestation of Black self-hatred. It is the crown jewel of the NIGGER FACTOR. And make no mistakes, Amerikkka is the NIGGER factory, where "NIGGERS" are mass produced, crafted and assembled by the hands (Ideology) of European culture, in furtherance of white domination. Moreover, "NIGGER" in its operative modality, is like a virtual code word - in the manner of which is used - for instance, in hypnosis, where when mentioned the (hypnotized) subject is induced into a (mental) sleep-like state, and readily accepts the suggestions and instructions of the hypnotist.

NIGGER or NIGGA (whichever you choose) comes from the word NEGRO, which is essentially derived from its etymological root NECRO which means DEAD; a term (in this context) denoting Black peoples' (mental) death. Hence the term MENTACIDE - a word coined by warrior-scholar Bobby E. Wright to more accurately contextualize the mind state of the Black man after it has been murdered (by the white man). How did the white man murder the mind of the

Bobby E. Wright

Black man? Well, it was/is a systematic (mental) murder (by attrition) where, at the very inception of the slave system, the process of destroying Afrikan images, languages, concepts, names, spiritual systems, customs and, more significantly, the systems of social communalism, was set in motion, having intergenerational effects.

Thus, over five-hundred years later, the Afrikan has become virtually unrecognizable here in the wasteland of North Amerikkka and in the broader Diaspora (even on the Afrikan continent). The traditional images of Afrika, thus of Afrikans, were effectively subdued and supplanted by Europeans and their Euro-Arab cousins. They demonized Afrika and everything that springs forth from its greatness (including Afrikan peoples), while simultaneously superimposing their (white) images and cultural ideologies as superior. They invented the word NIGGER to degrade the Afrikan. And as a stamp of his/her mental demise.

On the slave plantations, the word "NIGGER" was often uttered while captured Afrikans were being brutally beaten, or raped, or murdered, etc., by the white man (or one of his colorful house

"niggers'). So, not only was/is the word indicative of Afrikans' mental death, but on a deeper level, its very utterance evokes those

hypnotized or (mentally) enslaved, to function on the commands of the European hypnotist (enslaver), even in the murder of other Afrikans. In fact, when NIGGER (dead) replaced NDUGU (Brother) it made it easier for vanquished or hypnotized Blacks to kill other Blacks/Brothers. NIG-GER indicates worthlessness. So, although many Blacks claim they've changed its meaning to denote

something more endearing, it still, however, in a pragmatic way, provides the apt segue (in the conscientious sense) for the remorseless murder and every other facet of aggression against one's own (Black) people.

Ever wondered why Black men seem to be so mightily imbued with the "I'll kill a nigga in a minute" attitude, and why said 'Killing Spirit' isn't directed at their REAL enemies: The White Oppressor? Well, warrior-scholar Dr. Bobby E. Wright cogently offers that:

"Blacks kill Blacks because they have never been trained to kill whites, therefore, it is outside their experience. Historically, the European system has encouraged the killing of Blacks, and since Blacks have been led to believe that they are part of the (white) psychopath's system, they simply follow the practice."

The established system in which Blacks find themselves is predicated on the ire for Afrikan culture. And the Blacks that are grossly brainwashed into a euro-centric thought pattern, behave accordingly. However, to be-lieve the myth that Blacks are inherently prone to violence (especially against themselves) is to believe that the very womb of every Black wom-an is corrupt; For, certainly there is where every Black person is birthed from. And furthermore, it is to believe that the womb of mother Afrika is corrupt. Yet this is exactly what the white oppressor suggests in his por-trayal of Blacks in Amerikkkan literature, his tainted media machine, his pseudo Bell-Curve theories, etc. And tragically, many Blacks, in the ab-sence of their own cultural consciousness, are easily seduced into, what warrior-ancestor Dr. Amos N. Wilson called: *"The psycho-dynamics of Black self-annihilation in service of white domination."* Central to this dynamic is the fact that blacks (in a collective sense) have not developed the ability to effectively defend themselves from the (global) European onslaught. So, they naturally become frustrated. And this frustration is internalized and subsequently directed toward themselves. This is one of the main contributing factors in Blacks perpetuating violence against other Blacks.

The mystique concomitant with the system of white supremacy has taken up residence (in the perceptions of Blacks and other non-whites) as an omnipotent entity, "impregnable" and "insurmountable". And as long as Black people remain under the spell or hypnosis of the European ideologues who perpetuate such myths, they will forever be powerless!

Under European domination, Blacks are reduced to docile (cultural) cowards. It's like, for example, a man being chumped or emasculated in public, or on his job (by his superiors) only to go home and take out his frustrations on his wife or his family in general. His (acquired) cowardice precludes him from confronting the source of his frustration. And since all Afrikans, wherever they may be found on the planet, are essentially family (by extension of their common culture), the same logic applies to the fratricidal behavior that has become so common in the hood.

Charles Thorton

In this vein, we should point out an incident that took place in Kirkwood, Missouri some time ago, involving a Black man named Charles Thorton, who had endured blatant racist and discriminatory ordinances, by white city officials, against his self-owned asphalt business, incurring unjust fines & penalties, in an apparent effort to cripple his business. And when he filed complaints to reach some sort of amicable redress, he was rebuffed and summarily brushed off by local government officials. He didn't take it out on his family or community. Instead, he took counsel with his family who all agreed that City Hall was being run with a racist slave plantation mentality. So, he returned with his guns and declared war.

When the smoke cleared two (White) city council members, two (White) police officers, and the racist (White) mayor lay in pools of their own blood; with the mayor being the only survivor. Brother Charles Thorton was himself eventually gunned down by the police. And when interviewed by CNN, his brother Gerald Thorton told news reporters that his brother calmly and deliberately decided to take such course of action; Because he felt that the (White) rulers of this society have created an arrogant comfort zone, where they feel they can just arbitrarily, and with a sense of nonchalance, disrupt and disregard the lives of others (especially non-Whites) at their (racist) whim - with no repercussion. He wanted to show them that their lives could be disrupted as well; that their blood could be spilled, too; that every Black isn't necessarily controlled by the hypnotic NIGGER FACTOR. Moreover, he wanted to show other Blacks that whites aren't as invincible as they've deceived the world into believing.

"There is an anger that wakes up in you when you are a child and it builds up and determines the political consciousness of the Black man."

- WARRIOR ANCESTOR WINNIE MANDELA-

*** PILLARS OF SELF -HATRED ***

"The necessary re-education of Blacks and a possible solution of racial crisis can begin, strangely enough, only when Blacks fully realize this central fact in their lives: The white man Is their bitter enemy."

-WARRIOR ANCESTOR- SCHOLAR CHANCELLOR WILLIAMS-

IT IS EXTREMELY IMPORTANT for Blacks to understand the dynamics of white supremacy so that they can fully discern its inherent intentions, methods, nuances and affects upon its non-white subjects. To neglect this critical analysis is to continue to wander heedlessly into the fog of confusion wrought by its inherent hypocrisy. In this vein, it should first be understood that the system of white supremacy, by its very title, delineates its Manifest Destiny, at the obvious exclusion of Black and other nonwhite people.

So, for Blacks to continue to seek integration or any other form of amalgamation into such a system is to welcome or invite their own subjugation. Quite frankly, it brings into question the sanity of Black people. After all, what sane group of people would continuously fight to be the footstool of another (hostile) group of people? Only those who are mentally, culturally and spiritually impaired. The reality is, whites will never see Blacks as equals. For the matrix of white superiority is buttressed on the degradation of non-white peoples and their respective cultural imperatives.

Tragically, Blacks seem to think that white racism is a mere social defect that can be remedied through political participation or through the (false) notion of some omnipotent god (up in the sky). This line of puerile reasoning tends to (conveniently) ignore the controlling nature of Europeans' cultural thought and behavioral patterns, both historically and in the now-times.

White racism isn't some paroxysm that rears its 'ugly head' in isolated incidents like the Don Imus or Michael Richards or Dog the Bounty Hunter fiascos. It is the natural outgrowth of Europeans' cultural imperatives. To explicate the innate (and tactical) hypocrisy of whites, warrior Messenger Elijah Muhammad has warned that, when it serves the overall interests of whites, they make foisted proclamations that "color doesn't matter ', that "we' re all God's children" and the like. Nonetheless, in instances where such lies are ineffective in achieving their means, the same cross they claim that Jesus died on (for all our sins), that they claim is sacred, gets burned on your front lawn; to let you know: '"nigger" if you don't go along with our program of (of white domination) you'll burn just like this cross.' Or, as the Natives always say: "*The pale man speaks with forked tongue.*"Better yet, our Warrior-Scholar Sister Marimba Ani puts it in proper context when she termed the (hypocritical) double-speak of Europeans as their "Rhetorical Ethic" which she defines as: "*Culturally structured European hypocrisy. It is a statement framed in terms of acceptable moral behavior towards others that is meant for rhetorical purposes only. Its purpose is to disarm intended victims of European cultural and political imperialism. It is meant for "export" only. It is not intended to have significance within the culture. Its essence is Its deceptive effect in the service of European power.*"

It is the neglect to deal with Europeans and their cultural impositions in light of their "Rhetorical Ethic" factor, that has caused much disappointment and despair for those Blacks who

are entangled within the conceptual morass of euro-centric cultural hypocrisy. And within the parameters of this beguiling (cultural) framework, doing the 'right' thing is equivalent to doing the 'white' thing.

Additionally, with European culture being projected as the paragon of all that is lofty & excellent (as a 'universal' worldview), it is not surprising to see (vanquished) Blacks worshiping whites in every sector of sociological endeavor. It has therefore become common for Blacks to take pride in and celebrate the accolades bestowed upon them by 'benevolent' whites; often for some super inflated nothingness, performed within the confines of white folks' myopic worldview. Also, Blacks in this suspended mind frame can't seem to grasp the absurdity in their (relegated) claims of being the "first" to have reached some trite & inconsequential achievement in the field of some mundane endeavor; with whites being the standard bearers of course.

It is painful to conscious-minded Blacks to see their vanquished brethren instilled with (misplaced) pride to, for instance, boast being the "first" Black to be trusted to mow the White House lawn; The "first" to be accepted in an all-white school; The "first" to play in major league baseball; The "first" to win an Oscar, and a bunch of other asinine "firsts", as if whites are the shoe-in for greatness and Blacks are the exception. Moreover, it's as if Blacks' talents, intelligence, ability to achieve, etc. doesn't exist unless recognized by whites; or, as if Blacks are automatically assumed to be inherently inept, and therefore, anything they do (at white folks' par) is regarded with awe & wonder, as if witnessing something outside the realm of normal human capability in the manner of let's say, for example, witnessing a monkey play the violin. It is, quite frankly, the most sickening display of 'Niggativity'. a macabre of psycho-cultural death for sure.

Kenneth & Mamie Clark

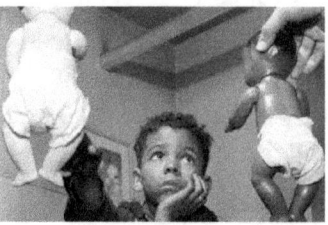

The Doll Test 1940

And in light of this minced mind state, which marks almost every aspect of Black people's social existence, it is little wonder then, why, when given the "Doll Test", Black children almost invariably choose the white doll as being the most Likeable, Innocent, Beautiful, Pure and the like. This isn't a disconnected condition. Black children are born into an environment of "Niggativity", so they merely reflect what's resonant in the (cultural) atmosphere.

The Doll Test 2015

Then there's the open worship of European fashion, which is tantamount to worshiping whites themselves. And true to form, there isn't a single Black fashion brand that is regarded (by Blacks) above those of Europeans': Versace, Gucci, Louis Vuitton, Prada, Dolce & Gabbana, Marc Jacobs, Polo and countless others. These are literally worshiped and deemed, by Blacks, as "Must-Haves". Even worse, Blacks think so little of themselves that many measure their self-worth by the acquisition and accumulation of all things European.

There is even an atmosphere of peer-pressure among Black people (especially in Hip-Hop culture) which promotes and reinforces this. One is literally considered un-cool if s/he isn't draped in the latest and 'most expensive' trappings of everything European. Interestingly, some European fashion designers have actually gone on record saying (explicitly) that they make their clothes and related accesso-

ries (exclusively) for whites - to stave off the gross deval-
uation of their respective brands, by their popularity in
the slums of urban centers. Ralph Lauren (Polo) and
Tommy Hilfiger have done this some years ago; then later
recanted (in the interest of consumer capital gains). The
champagne brand Cristal has done this as well. Yet Blacks
persist in the glorification of these (white) brands.

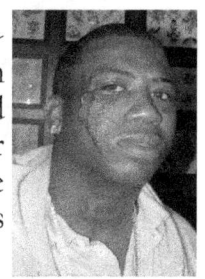

Guicci Mane

Even further, it isn't uncommon to find Blacks who
have even taken on these European-brand names (as
their own), to be, in some skewed way, associated with wealth (worth),
to escape their own Afrikan "worthlessness". In a more broader view, this
inverted notion encompasses European (slave masters')
names in general. Still, vanquished "negroes" (rhetorically)
maintain that a name is just a name devoid of any cultural
or historical (ourstorical) significance.

This carries over (in a broader sense) with bourgeois Blacks
literally speaking in white folk vernacular. In fact, it is common (in the Black colony) for those "negroes "who speak
with the king's perfect (English) tongue, to be openly criticized for "speaking like they're white". And while those
"negroes" on the receiving end of such criticism uniformly retort that such criticism is "really" a mindless aspersion cast by the "ignorant" and
"uneducated" upon their high levels of academic
achievements, they, however, completely miss or simply trivialize the
real point. Within the criticism what is really meant is that their phonetic cadence, their clipped, succinct, nasal pronunciation and lexicon,
marked by their syntactical pedantry along with their 'nose in the air'
style mannerisms, is like that of whites.

Kanye West aka

Louis Vuitton Don

Moreover, the overall content and context of their spiel shows them to
be loyal spokespersons of the very white-dominated system which op-
presses Blacks. Minister Alif (of the UNOI), Sister Minister Ava Muhammad. Amos N. Wilson, Queen Mother Audley Moore, Minister Louis
Farrakhan, the teenage academic phenom Autumn Ashante and a throng
of other Blacks who are known for their sharp and proficient oratory
skills, have never been accused or criticized (by the Black colony) for
'speaking like white folks. The "educated" versus the "uneducated' assertion (as the standing rebuttal) certainly isn't the case. The thing is, there

is an expressed resentment within the Black community, for those bourgeois negroes who hold themselves above their own people based (solely) on their "achievements" in Euro-Amerikkkan academia (to serve the perpetuation of white rule); especially those boasting their "degrees", which flaunts their hollow stature and proximity to their white masters. Warrior-Messenger Elijah Muhammad once stated, with regards to such "negroes", that: *"They are one-hundred percent poisoned in mind and into the love of the Devil (the white man)."*

Queen Mother Moore

However, such treasonous behavior isn't new. In the days of chattel slavery, the white slave master always kept a few "trusted" slaves close to him. These were called "House-Niggers". And they took great pleasure in being close to their white masters. They would often come around the enslaved Afrikans who worked the fields, to show off the second-hand clothes and other trinkets they were given by their masters; as well as the few "fancy" words they'd picked up from being in the presence of their masters. And because of this, they considered themselves better than those in the field. This mentality is still alive and well today.

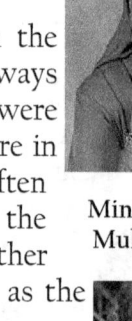

Minister Ava Muhammad

It is also common to see these euro-centric (cloned) "negroes" boast their multilingualism, in terms of their ability to speak several (European) languages, as well as their travels to the places where said languages are endemic. Yet, they not only neglect to (re)learn their own original (Afrikan) tongue, but they even ridicule Afrikan languages (in the manner of their white masters). Furthermore, they regard them as obsolete - as they do Afrikan peoples.

Autumn Ashante

Afrikan people inherently speak from their center (the soul). Whites, conversely, speak straight from the larynx (they have no soul). And, despite the so-called "educated negroes" attempts to trivialize or downplay it, there is a difference. And this difference is a rudiment indicator of the more broader polarities between

Europeans and Afrikans. So, when you see Blacks 'speaking' and acting like whites you're witnessing the victims of cultural imperialism; you're witnessing Blacks in retreat from their own Blackness, thus you're witnessing Black self-hatred.

"In the very syntax of our speech as we learn the English language, the justification of our 'inferiority' is embedded, and we accept that fact as we 'master' the language." - DR. MARIMBA ANI -

Dr. Marimba

These and other pillars of Black self-hatred are stifling factors, even facilitating elements, which normalizes Black powerlessness. Self-hatred is not natural; and doesn't just appear in a vacuum, out of thin air. Such an inverted (psychological) condition and resulting patterns of behavior had to have come from somewhere (outside one's innate will construct). Therefore, the source has to be identified, without trepidation, in order to effectively remove the spell of Black-inferiority, thus, white domination.

This isn't an argument of 'Rights' & 'Wrongs', in terms of methods, as defined within the confines of euro-centric thought) or monopolized by Europeans "Rhetorical Ethic"; but rather a move toward Black Liberation, Black Power, from an Afrikan-centered paradigm. That which is 'Right' for whites is apparently 'Wrong' for Blacks (as evinced in the disparate power dynamics between the two races). Likewise, that which is 'Right' for Blacks (pursuant to Black Power) is 'Wrong' for whites. That which is a lie to Blacks is their truth. And those Blacks who are loyal adherents to that lie are "NIGGERS" and are agents of the purveyors of the lie, thus the liars and enemies of Black Liberation, Black Power. Such are the demarcation lines in the theater of cultural war!

The inexorable pursuit of real, tangible Black Power should be the mission of conscious Blacks (globally). Because to merely be (culturally) conscious under white domination simply isn't going to cut it. By nature, one's cultural spirit and behavior has to have (unimpeded) space to thrive and fully express itself; a space or territory governed by Afrikan people and defended by Afrikan warriors. A culture minus the ability to fluently express itself is vulnerable, thus susceptible to the whims of the dominant elements of the prevailing culture. and since European culture is a warmonger culture, war (with them) is inevitable. So, if Blacks are not engaged in battle (on our respective frontiers) we're engaged in capitulation or treason; plain & simple.

Anything not in a state of motion or growth is either in a state of decay or is simply dormant, thus useless. Well, the same applies to Black struggle. Our growth and perpetuity (as Afrikans) rests upon our active engagement in war and struggle. Our mission has to be (without any ambiguities) geared toward establishing a Black power base; and ushered into existence by courageous Pan-Afrikan warriors. And Afrikan culture has to be both the healing balm and the binding element, to ensure victory. In this vein' it is necessary to point out that:

"The study of the history of national liberation struggles shows generally these struggles are preceded by an increase in the expression of culture, consolidated progressively into a successful attempt to affirm the cultural personality of the dominated people, as a means of negating the oppressor culture. Whatever may be the conditions of the people's political and social factors in practicing this domination, it is generally within the culture that we find the seed of opposition, which leads to the structuring and developing of the liberation movement.... The fact that independence movements are generally marked, even in their early stages, by an upsurge of cultural activity, has led to the view that such movements are preceded by a 'cultural 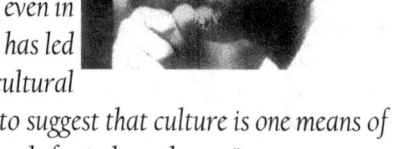 *renaissance' of the subject people. Some go so far as to suggest that culture is one means of collecting together a group, even a weapon in the struggle for independence."*

-WARRIOR -ANCESTOR-SCHOLAR AMILCAR CABRAL -

The Black youth need to be trained & organized to be the (new) leaders of the revolution that is looming on the horizon. They are (rightfully) fed up with lackey Black leadership and their "Politically Correct" rhetoric to "Stop the Violence". The Black youth are violent for a reason, just against the wrong target

(themselves). So, a radical re-education (ReAfrikanization) is in order. The revolution calls for the re-focusing and re-directing of the violence (not "Stop the Violence"). The violence needs to be harnessed to the extent of advancing and protecting the interests of Afrikans, and the implementation of their socio-political agenda, both defensively and offensively.

The many street-fraternities (so-called gangs) that have sprung up throughout the Black colony show great potential. However, in the past, when they were called to organize in truces they came together, only to be given lip-service steeped in reform rhetoric or some religious mumbo-jumbo, to quell the capitalist oppressor's fears. That is, until the NATIONAL BLACK LEGATEE ASSOCIATION, THE BLACK RIDERS LIBERATION PARTY, THE ASAFO YA UHURU and other revolutionary formations stepped up.

No Afrikan trapped in the hells of North Amerikkka can (in good conscience) deny that revolution is in the air. After all, what can be said of the mass disinterest in the capitalist oppressor's inferior educational system, thus the increasing drop-out rate; The ostensible self-hatred, manifested in Black-on-Black violence and

other (Black) self-destructive practices which, as if on cue, is (ignorantly) glorified in today's rap music, hood novels, straight-to-video movies, etc.; The routine murder of unarmed Blacks, and the police-state style occupation of the Black colony by the racist & repressive police apparatus; The spreading of HIV/AIDS in the Black colony; The mindless gang and drug culture concomitant with the soaring incarceration rates of Black and other non-White men (and women); The growing joblessness & homeless rates; etc.

The "negro" politicians and the treasonous religious leaders (especially those selected and employed by former president Bush's *Faith-Based Initiative*) have to be exposed as collaborators with our open enemies. They have to be strongly opposed. For they have been allowed (by the people) to promote the oppressor's nefarious politics and disempowering religious ideologies, etc. They are largely responsible for the maintenance of the Black masses' socio-political attenuation.

Even in this critical epoch of, what warrior Messenger Elijah Muhammad called: "*The Day of Decision*" lackey Black leaders are begging white Amerikkka for palliate accommodations and empty, insincere apologies for the Afrikan Maafa (the continued destruction of Afrikan peoples) - which is tantamount to, what warrior Minister Malcolm X once explained as: "*A man pushing a knife six inches into your back then pulling it out three inches and calling that justice.*" Not to mention that he stabbed you in the first place.

Minister Malcolm X

In conclusion, it is noteworthy to mention that, every chance they get, and wherever they can find an ear or the attention of the world at large, the Zionist so-called Jews tell their 'holocaust' story, suffered at the hands of Hitler's Nazi regime; and have vowed "Never Again!" In fact, they're still hunting down Nazi war criminals (as we speak), to be punished for alleged crimes committed against them. And they pass this legacy, burden and responsibility down to their children, so on & so forth. Yet these very same people (arrogantly) admonish Blacks to "Stop Blaming the White Man" for the much more devastating and far-reaching 'hell-a-caust' the white man (including so-called Jews) perpetrated against Afrikans, with the lingering effects being felt in the present. They have even convinced vanquished Blacks to "Get Over It". This is blasphemy to any self-respecting Afrikan. It's time to RISE UP!

"The potential for the ascension of the fighting spirit in Blacks is great. But its viability and strength must be carefully directed, for maximum effect. The formation of a (secret) Black warrior priesthood is of paramount Importance to the establishment and protection of an Afrikan-centered social system. Secrecy is its strength. conversely, where secrecy is neglected we will see the tenuity of the entire formation. Therefore, the snitch factor. should be rooted out and eliminated."

- MCHUMA JICHO, NBLA-

** NAME WARS: CLASH OF THE TITLES **

"When we get ready to create revolution we must redefine the world and redefine words; there's no way around it. In Genesis, we see Adam being given the power to name things. Through being given the power to name things he is given dominion. There is a connection between naming and dominion, between naming and bringing things into reality. When we permit another people to name and define, we permit another people to gain dominion and control over us. - **DR. AMOS N. WILSON**-

MANY PEOPLE in this (Amerikkkan) society tend not to give any serious thought to their name, its origins, ancestral connection or definition (within its cultural context), respectively.

This is especially true of Black people. In fact, it is an alarming anomaly that Blacks (in particular) don't seem to mind what they are called or what they call themselves; though, ironically, they tend to identify themselves by what they are called (by others), no matter the cultural insignificance or pejorative connotation, as if a name is just a dead word, devoid of any tangible bearing beyond its verbal or audible utterance.

A telling sign for sure, of Black people's cultural destitution and disconnectedness. It is common knowledge that the Euro-Amerikkkan slave system is directly responsible for forcefully and systematically dispossessing (kidnapped) Afrikans of their original names, which was done to spiritually, psychologically and culturally demoralize them; to, in effect, cut off their cultural umbilical cord, thus hurling them into an abominable state of amnesia, which reverberated from generation to generation up to the now-times, which leads us to the important question of:

IF THERE WASN'T ANY SIGNIFICANCE TO NAMES THEN WHY
WERE SUCH PAINSTAKING MEASURES AND METHODS EM-
PLOYED BY EUROPEANS TO WREST THEM FROM THEIR
AFRIKAN CAPTIVES?

The European captors understood the psychological affects it would have, in terms of disempowering their Afrikan captives, to better facilitate their subjugation. It also served to further empower the white captors, to solidify their dominance. Moreover, the changing of Afrikans' names was one of the most paramount sequences of the entire system of captivity and enslavement; for it imbued the white captors with the spirit of "legitimate" proprietorship relative to their human "property". Hence, renaming Afrikans was/is the most telling method to reflect such.

In Alex Haley's made-for-TV mini-series ROOTS, a glimpse into the re-naming process, albeit a pabulum version, was illustrated when the (Afrikan) character Kunta Kente was brutally beaten while being commanded by the white slave maker to denounce his REAL (Afrikan) name and to openly accept/announce his newly given (slave) name "Toby". And while a (mainstream) highlight is often shone on the fact that, after a near-death beating, he eventually succumbed, little attention is given to the fact that he resisted for as long as he possibly could, just short of succumbing to physical death itself. And in that context, the scene captured the importance and significance of the Afrikan's connection to his name, as well as the European slave maker's resolve to remove it from him. Surely Kunta Kente went to war for his name (identity) without a weapon the equal of his adversary's; Only His Will to Resist! An Afrikan warrior woman once proclaimed that: *"To divest an Afrikan of his or her name is equivalent to decapitation; for without one's name, just like a body without its head, one roams heedlessly (without purpose) and die namelessly (without identity)."*

Alex Haley

Kunta Kinte'

Sadly, in the now times, Blacks can be called anything - even Amerikkkan - without so much as a question, much less resistance. In fact, Afrikans of today, especially here in Amerikkka, don't even consider themselves Afrikan. They have been misled, through the gross manipulation of history, by Europeans, that: "It ain't where you're from its where you're at." And to this dense line of reasoning, Malcolm X once quipped that: *"If a cat had kittens in an oven you wouldn't call 'em muffins."* The same logic applies to Afrikans here in Amerikkka (and elsewhere in the Diaspora).

If, for instance, one was to see a polar bear in the (Arctic) North Pole (its original habitat) or see one in captivity (in your local zoo or the like), it's still a Polar Bear; even if its captors decide to name it something else. Its essential identity isn't relinquished simply because it is removed from its original domicile. And its off-spring - whether born at home or in captivity - is still of Polar descent.

Likewise, the term "African-American" is a misnomer. The proper order would be Afrikan (in Amerikkka). Furthermore, Afrikans (in Amerikkka) bearing Euro-Amerikkkan names are just as insidious. In reality, for an Afrikan to be out of his/her name is indicative of him or her being out of their (natural) mind. The Afrikan name isn't just a word existing in a state of suspended animation, as regarded in the western world view. Conversely, it is the working, functional title or motivating force of one's consciousness, and (personal) source of self-empowerment. It is the core characteristic of one's being, one's purpose, etc. (within the collectivity of the Afrikan community).

The very phonetic inflections of traditional Afrikan languages have a cohesive and harmonious congruence with the very universe we inhabit (cosmologically). And on an even deeper level, their very ineffable rhythmic vibrations are intrinsically encoded in the molecular structure of the high concentration levels of melanin that is (exclusively) endemic to Afrikan peoples. And said, 'rhythmic vibrations' were (once upon a time) an inaudible method of communication among ancient Afrikans who were so in tuned with each other. Such a "phenomenon" is what is considered today to be Extra Sensory Perception (E.S.P.).

Furthermore, Afrikan languages are the (audible) configuration of the first sounds made/heard in the sphere of audio-transmission and constructed into intelligible forms of communication; even through physical objects/instruments, i.e., the akoben (war horn), the drum, etc. And, traditionally, the names chosen from the languages belonging to Afrika are one with Afrikan consciousness.

In fact, an Afrikan's name is his/her first (personal) truth, which informs his/her life's actions. It also reflects in his/her physical being - illuminating in his/her very countenance an (inherited) wisdom that is essentially derived from the truth and power of his/her name. Biblical scriptures put it thusly:

"A man's wisdom maketh his face to shine, and the boldness of his face shall be changed."   - ECCLESIASTES 8:1 -

Also, Warrior Messenger Elijah Muhammad has put forth that:

"One of the first and most important truths that must be established in this day is our identity."

A powerful name imbues one's consciousness with power, which in turn has a bearing on one's physical and other behavioral characteristics, which are reflected in the reciprocal interactions of (conscious-minded) Afrikans. In traditional (unpolluted/pre-colonialized) Afrikan society, one was held to the letter or definition) of his/her name. In this context, for example, if one's name was Balagoon (meaning warrior) or Duguma (meaning Spear), it was expected of him/her to perform in that capacity, in protection of the society or respective enclave, as well as the society's interests, whether physically, materially, spiritually or what have you. A nomenclature (if you will). And the society (as a collective) would act as a facilitating agency or milieu for the growth & development and full manifestation of one's destiny, which is essentially ensconced within his/her name. For the name is a container, representing the sum of its contents or definition. So, one is (in pragmatic terms) what s/he is identified or called by; the name being inextricable from the character or behavior of the individual (as it pertains to one's standing within the collective).

This tradition of repatriation/re- Afrikanization was revitalized within the Nation of Islam (under Mr. Elijah Muhammad), as with other Pan-Afrikan/ Black Cultural-Nationalist movements throughout Amerikkka (and beyond). It has, in fact, become the hallmark of the Afrikan re-awakening. And it is in this tradition that Wesley Cook became Mumia Abu-Jamal, H. Rap Brown became Jamil Al-Amin, Larry Crawford became Mwalimu Bomani Baruti, Stokely Carmichael became Kwame Ture, Arthur Commeger became Minister Khallid Alif Allah, Louis Walcott became Minister Louis Farrakhan, Dona Richards became Marimba Ani, Joanne Chesimard became Assata Shakur, Gary Graham became Shaka Sankofa, Harold Moore became Dr. Khallid Muhammad, Malcolm Little became Malcolm X (later El-Hajj Malik El-Shabazz) and finally (before his death) Omowale. And the list goes on. And while this warrior tradition signifies the breaking of the white man's power (over oneself), it also, in the eyes of whites, represents a blatant act of defiance, an open threat to white domination; because the name change is indicative of a Neo-Liberated, self-empowered consciousness that runs counter to being dominated by any foreign culture, or any other alien entity. Thus war (of the names, titles, designations, etc.) is inevitable.

"Even these (white) people recognize that a name is connected to a social role. A name is not just something you call people, but the name a people are called signifies their role. Therefore, a change of name represents a people's attempt to change their role and

position in the world. Some 'negroes' think that to change our name is just some foolish game we're playing. It's not about that. Even other people recognize that."

– WARRIOR-ANCESTOR- SCHOLAR DR. AMOS N. WILSON-

Europeans have a (power fueled) fetish for (re)naming thus redefining everything (and everybody) within their warped sphere of (imperial) reach. This goes hand in hand with innate need to dominate everything and everybody.

When Elijah Poole first (publicly) became ELIJAH MUHAMMAD he was harassed by the FBI. They even sought to arrest him (for forgery), for signing MUHAMMAD instead of Poole. He boldly told them that he didn't need theirs or any other repressive government agency's permission to use a name that was given to him by God. And, despite their threats to arrest him (if he continued), he never stopped signing or going by MUHAMMAD. It is said that the first step in breaking the spell or influence of white domination is to simply disobey it. Warrior Messenger Elijah Muhammad disobeyed. And the white man eventually acquiesced and was forced to address him as MUHAMMAD.

Afrikans (in Amerikkka) who return to their culture, thus their original names, often have said names relegated to wanton illegitimacy relative to the colonial "Government-Name" or "Slave-Name" that was denounced. For example, recently, while reading. a piece on Malcolm X (for Black History Month), the (white) writer said that: "Although he is widely known as Malcolm X, his REAL name is Malcolm Little" - with REAL being the salient implication - as if his (slave) surname is REAL and its repudiation, as indicated by the" X", a name of his own choosing, isn't legitimate.

Tragically, ignorant "neqroes" still follow in this (European-centered) tradition. This is the same tradition in which Afrikans were/are called "Negro", "Nigger", "Colored", "Afro-Amerikkkan", etc. by whites; all of which are embraced, accepted and utilized by Blacks, representing their mental & cultural enslavement.

In fact, (mentally) enslaved "negroes" detest the very mention of anything BLACK or AFRIKAN. For their minds have been thoroughly baptized in euro-centric ideology, influence and white domination. Moreover, such an "other directed" individual is the by-product of white supremacy (a "negro"); s/he is the brainchild of cultural imperialism. Therefore, s/he isn't allowed to THINK, FEEL, SPEAK or BEHAVE outside the circumference of euro-centric dominance. Because to do so is to be accused of "Hating White People" - as if this is the sole reason for the bold & radical reclamation of one's true Afrikan self, as if it's perfectly normal for Afrikans to behave like Europeans. Afrikans don't hate Europeans. Afrikans hate European imperial domination and institutionalized white racism. Blacks don't hate whites simply because they're white. Blacks hate that whites want every other people to think & function from a white-centered paradigm. European culture doesn't stand on its own hollow merits (within the universal world view). It is buttressed on the demonization of others' cultures, which is the handmaiden of its hegemonic aggressions.

A quick glance around this (stolen) land (Amerikkka) will certainly reveal how they have shaped (named) it in their (continental) European image. For instance, NEW York, NEW England, NEW Hampshire, NEW Haven, NEW Jersey, NEW Castle, etc., is a clear indication that there must be an OLD: York, Hampshire, Haven, Jersey & castle in old England. The very name AMERICA comes from the European "explorer" Americus Vespucci. And the capitol district (Columbia) is named for Christopher Columbus; with the State itself (Washington) being named for George Washington.

This (Imperialist) trend has even become pervasive on the continent of Africa. The capitol of Liberia, a so-called "independent" African state, established by "Freed Slaves", is named Monrovia, in honor of the 5th United States president, James Monroe. Zimbabwe is formerly Rhodesia, named for Cecil J. Rhodes. Alexandria, Egypt is named for the European invader Alexander "the great". In fact, the very name EGYPT itself is of Greek origin and isn't really the name of that (African) region. Its original name (among many) is KEMET.

The European name beset upon Afrika represents conquest, colonialism, (white) domination and ultimately disrespect, thus war! And for any Afrikan to submit to such is to willingly relinquish one's own cultural armor and empowerment. Blacks (Afrikans) must reject white (European) names, titles, labels, designations, etc.; especially one of the most infamous & damning cognomens in the arsenal of white supremacist insults: "Nigger"; or its variables, "Nigga", "Negro", etc. For, such an epithet designates one's past to the wasteland of nothingness. English is connected to England. French to France. Spanish to Spain. Negro/Nigger to nothing.

"Put simply, we should call ourselves in the language our ancestors will understand, not some tongue foreign to them. If they do not understand us, they cannot aid us. Moreover, to name ourselves, without asking others' permission or apologizing for being ourselves, is to be powerful." — MWALIMU BARUTI —

Afrikans, wherever they may be located in the Global Diaspora, are belonging to Afrika. Therefore, their names (and ways) should be reflective of such. Ironically, many continental Africans, from the onset of European colonialism, have become bereft of their original or traditional customs, names, practices, etc. For instance, in the north-west Afrikan country of Algeria, you will find that a lot of the native Afrikans speak French (exclusively) and bear French names. The sure markings of French occupation and influence.

The Congo (formerly Zaire), though a so-called autonomous Afrikan nation-state, still bears vestiges of Belgian (colonial) rule & influence. Also, the former French colony Haiti, an island-nation in the West Indies, laden predominantly with Afrikans, though over two-hundred years up from French subjugation, is still submerged in French names, customs, etc. The same is true of Afrikans here in Amerikkka, who are almost two-hundred years up from chattel slavery yet still go in the names (and behaviors) of their European enslavers.

Interestingly though, and, albeit at a lethargic pace, the Sankofa/Re-Afrikanization Movement is underway (universally). However, Afrikans in the western hemisphere, particularly in Amerikkka, are at the fore-front of this movement. And as Afrikans (the world over) begin to re-claim their traditions, thus their rightful place within the universal order of things; they'll inevitably select names that are indicative of STRENGTH & WARRIORHOOD - pursuant to their collective Liberation. For they are consciously and actively stepping from beneath the pall of Eurocentric designation and re-connecting with their warrior-ancestors. The old Euro-Amerikkkan saying - *"Go in the world and make a NAME for yourselves."*

My poor blind, deaf and dumb people are going by the wrong names and until you ac-cept the truth of your true identity and accept the names of your people and nation we will never be respected because of this alone. This is one of the reasons Almighty Allah has come among us, that is to give us His Names, the Most Holy and Righteous Names of the planet Earth."

- WARRIOR MESSENGER ELIJAH MUHAMMAD -

It should always be remembered that we are, whether we contend or not, engaged in a (name) war. Names are words that have the power to cause action (or not), For example, if one is constantly being referred to as "Nigger/Nigga", which essentially means dead, then one will remain inac-tive in the face of every other facet of European (or any other foreign) aggression, as the name itself is lifeless.

Moreover, to function in a European name (mind-set) could cause one to act against one's own self & ilk, in the interest of one's European enslav-ers. Conversely, to be in one's own Afrikan name (consciousness) is to be in-tune with one's inherent strength, and (naturally) aligned with one's universal brotherhood. One also has the ability to readily discern any for-eign threats or encroachments on one's person, group or culture in gen-eral, both internally and externally.

Afrikans (traditionally) function according to the universal principles of MAAT, which are: TRUTH, ORDER, JUSTICE, BALANCE, HARMO-NY, and RIGHTEOUSNESS & RECIPROCITY. And so, there is never a contradiction between what an Afrikan THINKS, SAYS & DOES. This powerful tradition is inextricably connected to the Afrikan principle of NOMMO, which deals with the power of words and the ability to speak them into (material) manifestation. For words are audible thoughts transmitted into the atmosphere, to be inculcated into human conscious-ness, to in effect provoke action. And names come in the same vein. Hence, there is power encoded in a name. *"A good NAME Is rather to be cho-sen than great riches, and loving favor rather than silver and gold."*

- PROVERBS, 22:1-

*** THE 'X' FACTOR ***

WARRIOR-MESSENGER ELIJAH MUHAMMAD, one of the most unsung Black leaders to emerge from the hells of North Amerikkka, is one of the first to address (among other things) the importance of discarding the white man's name, and the reclamation of traditional names. And since the first converts to his burgeoning Black Muslim Movement were so submerged in the muck of European dominance, thereby devoid of their customs, languages, names, etc. their slave surnames were summarily replaced with an 'X', as a sort of quasi-divorce from being recognized or identified as the white slave makers' property. The 'X' in the Black Muslim's "Supreme Alphabet" lessons means UNKNOWN, symbolizing that the Black man had been ripped from his ancestral surname, rendering said name UNKNOWN. The 'X' also serves as an interim or transitional name, to give the newly awakened time to divest themselves of European -induced thinking and behaviors, to be fit to be given a new name/attribute consistent with their new mission and way of life.

Contrary to popular belief, it isn't a trite novelty or some frivolous whim, with regards to Blacks making the conscious decision to reclaim their traditional names/identity. In fact, it is a necessary requisite in strengthening one's psycho-cultural immune system. For it is one's functional, kinetic connection to PAST, PRESENT & FUTURE simultaneously. It is identity & destiny all rolled into one (so to speak). Moreover, it is literally a matter of (cultural) LIFE or DEATH. RULE or be RULED!

"It is no big secret that the white rulers of any society under their control engages heavily in the manipulation of words, names, contexts, terms, phrases & titles as an agency of ideological warfare, to ensure and maintain the psychological subjugation of the subject group (s). Therefore, the warrior-class from among the New-Afrikan community or the ASAFO YA UHURU (Warriors of Freedom) must engage the ideologues of Yurugu's army on the psycho-cultural frontier and defeat them!"
- IRON EYE-

NEVER FORGET

NEVER FORGET:

History's blood-stained pages, the slave ships, the pale rage, the Black auction-blocks, how MUMIA was framed, the land stolen from the natives and the MOVE bombing on Osage ...

NEVER FORGET:

The trees from which Black spirits still swing, the forty-one shots from racist cops, the BRAVE-HEARTS buried at Wounded Knee and the savage beating of Rodney King ...

NEVER FORGET:

Sojourner's Truth. Steve Bico, Noble Drew, Franz Fanon, Nat Turner and Harriet Tubman's escape route ...

NEVER FORGET:

Khalid Muhammad's mysterious demise. Why Garvey's vision was blinded by white lies and how Medgar Evers' blood was poured into our eyes ...

NEVER FORGET:

The White-Knights. the burning crosses, EMMETT TILL. the Black boycotts and strikes, ROSA PARKS; Seeking Civil Rights from un-civilized whites. All cloaked in Red. White & Blue stripes ...

NEVER FORGET:

J. Edgar Hoover. His COINTELRPO maneuvers. How they popped Fred Hampton & Huey Newton, Malcolm and Martin Luther ...

NEVER FORGET:

The C.I.A. 'S abduction of the Prince of the Jungle, Patrice Lumumba. The assassinations of: Che Guevara, George Jackson and Bunchy Carter

NEVER FORGET:

The exiled Queen Assata, Clarence 13 "The Father", ELIJAH and white Amerikkka's fear of a BLACK MESSIAH.

ALSO FROM LEGATEE INK PUBLISHING

LET THE CIPHER OF SILENCE BE UNBROKEN

By Asafo Chuma Asafo

25 Years Enslaved

A Pennsylvania Prisoner's Appeal for Freedom

By

Robert Asafo Williams

PRINTED AND PUBLISHED BY:

LEGATEE INK PUBLISHING

1623 Dalton Street #14939

Cincinnati, Ohio 45250

Queen Tahiyrah Layout & Illustrations

LEGATEE INK PUBLISHING 2018